The

A little book of lavatorial humour and other bumf!

COMPILED BY

David Brown

Michael O'Mara Books Limited

This edition published in Great Britain in 2002 by
Michael O'Mara Books Limited
9 Lion Yard, Tremadoc Road
London SW4 7NQ

A CIP catalogue record for this book is available from
the British Library

ISBN 1-85479-456-6

1 3 5 7 9 10 8 6 4 2

Designed and typeset by Design 23
Printed in China

CONTENTS

*Beware of
draughty privys and of
pyssynng in draughts, and
permyt no common pyssynng
place about the house.*

MEDIEVAL SAYING

INTRODUCTION

Most people, when asked to name the invention that has most profoundly affected the course of modern civilization, would perhaps think first of the wheel, the airplane, the telephone, the television or the internet. However, while it might not be the most glamorous innovation, there is a strong case to be made for the toilet. Without it, and its accompanying waste treatment systems, living in towns and cities, such as London or Birmingham, with their high density of human population, would be all but impossible. Imagine thousands of people emptying their chamberpots in the street every morning – it would bring a new meaning to the phrase 'morning rush hour'!

As you now sit comfortably on your wooden or plastic toilet seat, it's worth remembering what your situation would have been like a mere 150 years ago. There would have been no light, no heating, no toilet paper, no seat to speak of and, most importantly, no water to wash everything away afterwards.

Banished to a rather decrepit lean-to shack at the bottom of the garden, and forced to sit on a scratchy piece of wood over a foul-smelling hole clutching some grass or leaves in your hand, you'd find yourself wishing that you never had to use the toilet again!

◆

There are countless curious and amusing facts about the history of the toilet, many of which will be revealed in this fascinating little book.

SETTING THE STANDARD

The first Englishman to have
had a toilet was probably the
Abbot of St Albans. Around
AD 1115 he built a stone cistern
to hold rainwater which he used
to flush his lavatory.

*O*ne Saturday in 1259 the 'Jew of Tewkesbury' fell into a privy pit and, out of respect for his Sabbath, no one was permitted to pull him out. On the Sunday, as a result of the Christian objections of the Bishop of Gloucester, his rescue was still not allowed. On Monday he was dead.

In the early fourteenth century,
Sherborne Lane in London
(once a beautiful stream)
became known as Shiteburn Lane
on account of the effect of its
overhanging latrines.

◆

In 1358 there were only
four public latrines in the
whole of London.

The men who emptied the cesspits in medieval times were called 'gongfermors' – 'gong' means a latrine or privy and 'fermor' derives from the verb to 'fey' meaning to cleanse.

◆

Pity the plight of poor Richard the Raker, who fell through the planks of a public latrine and drowned in the deep pit of excrement below.

*T*he great developments in the design of British loos were achieved by the creative impulse of a poet (in 1596), the meticulous skill of a watchmaker (in 1775), the practical mind of a cabinet-maker (in 1778) and the flair of a cook (in 1782). Not a single plumber!

*C*redit for inventing the first British flushing water closet is given to the poet and writer Sir John Harington, who in 1596 installed one in his house at Kelstone, near Bath, and another at Richmond Palace, for his godmother Queen Elizabeth I. However, it took more than 150 years for his invention to be developed or even copied.

The diagram of
Sir John Harington's pioneering
1596 WC at Kelstone shows a
cistern complete with fish
swimming in it.

There were over a hundred houses built on the original London Bridge, each with some sort of toilet arrangement with outflows directly into the Thames below. As a result, it was said that London Bridge was 'for wise men to go over and for fools to go under'.

Not a single patent for a
water closet of any kind was
taken out in the first 158 years
of British patents.

◆

The first British patent for a fully
operational flushing water closet
was taken out in 1775 by
Alexander Cumming, a Bond
Street watchmaker.

In 1778 Joseph Bramah perfected the flushing mechanism patented by Cumming and he went on to mass-produce a water closet which then remained the standard for nearly 100 years. However, by 1797 he had sold only 6,000 WCs – not many when you consider that the population of England was about eight million at the time.

After visiting the house of an acquaintance in 1760, Horace Walpole wrote, 'But of all curiosities, are the *conveniences* in every bedchamber: great mahogany projections ... with the holes, with brass handles, and cocks, &c. – I could not help saying, it was the *loosest* family I ever saw!'

*T*he Hopper was a particularly badly designed loo of the late 1790s. S. S. Hellyer, a talented sanitarian of those days, suggested an alternative use for them. 'Instead of destroying the thousands already made,' he wrote, 'they might be used by market gardeners for protecting rhubarb from frost.'

In 1793 a certain Mr Binns of Marylebone patented an automatic WC with a 'measurer' that filled with water when you sat down and flushed when you stood up.

A cartoon published in 1796 revealed both English pride in their water closet and contempt for other Europeans. It depicted the English with a water closet, the Scots with a bucket, the French with a latrine and the Dutch using a lake.

Many streets in British towns in the 1830s were floating with sewage. One street in Leeds, in which 176 families lived, was not cleaned at all for 15 years.

The pollution in the River Thames caused by sewage became particularly bad in the Victorian era. In 1858 'The Great Stink' from the Thames caused Parliament to close down.

*I*n the days before mains drainage, the night workmen who used to empty people's outside earth closets or privies were known as 'night-soil men' (also as 'honeycart men' or 'lavender-pickers'). There were still night-soil men employed in parts of Norfolk as recently as 1989.

The revolutionary penny-in-the-slot public loos at the Great Exhibition at Crystal Palace in 1851 were visited by 827,280 people and made a profit of £1,790 in 23 weeks.

One of the most popular chamber pots in the nineteenth century had a giant eye printed at the bottom with the words:

Use me well, and keep me clean
And I'll not tell what I have seen.

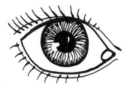

London's first men's public toilet with WCs opened in Fleet Street on 2nd February 1852. The first ladies' opened just off the Strand nine days later. Despite advertisements in *The Times* three times a week and 50,000 handbills, only 58 men and 24 women visited in the first month, and the experiment was abandoned.

The Earth Closet was invented in 1860 by Reverend Samuel Moule for places without piped water. It used a bucket, with a tank filled with dry earth or cinders at the back. When the lever was pulled, a measured amount of earth dropped into the bucket to cover the latest offering. Most 'green' loos of the twenty-first century also avoid the use of water.

In Victorian times, gentlemen's stand-up urinals sometimes bore a picture of a bee to aim at to prevent splashing. The reason for the bee is thought to be that the Latin word for bee is *apis*.

London's first proper drainage system, with 83 miles of large intercepting sewers, opened in 1865.

We owe the expression 'spending a penny' to George Jennings. Jennings built London's 'public conveniences', beginning in the 1870s, and was happy to supply and fix the appliances free of charge provided he was allowed to charge patrons a fee of one penny.

*T*homas Crapper (1836–1910) was a successful London plumber who was employed by the royal family to install new loos at Sandringham. He perfected the 'Valveless Water Waste Preventer' but, contrary to popular misconception, he did not invent the WC. The word 'crap', meaning defecate, does not derive from his name, as it has been in use since 1846, when Crapper was only ten years old.

Some brand names for manufacturers' toilets in the nineteenth and early twentieth centuries include The Deluge, The Torrent, The Rapidus, The Rocket, The Zone, The Axis, The Cardinal, The Improved Windermere, The Tornado, The Panorama, The Tubal and The Sultan.

*T*he privy or outhouse slowly became accepted, although in the early days they were often looked upon with a great deal of suspicion. One diarist wrote in disgust: "Privy houses set against ye Strete which spoiling people's apparill should they happen to be nare when ye filth comes out ... Especially in ye Night when people can not see to shun them."

*L*ike many members of the royal family, ordinary people developed the idea of the toilet as a status symbol. In colonial America, William Byrd's 1730 outhouse was made of brick and had five holes. Byrd was a chief magistrate and thus sat on the largest seat at the center of a raised, semicircular bench. Thus did Mr. Byrd preside in the family privy.

In aping the customs of the mother country, colonial Americans were very keen on upholding the tradition of 'taking the waters' in spas to cure various ailments. It was believed that the more foul-tasting the water, the more effective the cure. Dr. Benjamin Rush had the bad luck to have a well with horrible-tasting water in his backyard, to which the whole town flocked. When the over-pumped well went dry, the people learned too late that the well connected to the doctor's privy.

TOILETS
ABROAD

The Roman Emperor Vespasian
(ruled AD 69–79) imposed a tax on
the use of public urinals. Until
quite recently the *pissoirs* in France
used to be called 'Vespasiennes'
in his honour.

The Harappan culture in North-West India around 2,500 BC was probably the first civilization to have proper loos. The homes in the settlement of Mohenjo-Daro had privies connected to underground drains. It should be noted that the general sanitary arrangements in India today are no longer regarded as among the world's most advanced.

*A*bout 4,000 years ago the Palace of King Minos at Knossos on the island of Crete had toilets which flushed with rainwater using an ingenious system of pipes, and they also had wooden seats. In matters of sanitation, the Minoan civilization was far in advance of eighteenth-century Britain.

In ancient Rome they had gods to guard their toilets. Crepitus was god of the toilet and Cloacina was goddess of the common sewer. Public loos were called *cloaca* in her honour and Rome's main sewer was called the Cloaca Maxima.

In AD 315 there were 144 public toilets in Rome, most of which accommodated many people. The Roman settlement at Timgad in North Africa had a public loo for every 28 people – probably more than any town in Western Europe today.

Public loos in ancient Rome were very public indeed. There were no walls or partitions; sitters were in full view of any passer-by. Roman citizens regarded going to the toilet as something of a social event – they went there to meet their friends, have a chat and exchange news and gossip.

The British call the toilet 'the loo'. The French call it 'the little corner'. The ancient Egyptians called it 'the house of the morning'.

The first separate public toilets for men and women were established in a restaurant in Paris in 1739.

*B*efore the arrival of WCs, the privies in Japan were emptied regularly by men who *paid* for the right, since human waste represented a lot of money as fertilizer. Poor people could pay their rent with the proceeds from their waste.

Prior to India's independence, grandmothers in the province of Punjab used to eat the first excrement of a male child if he was born after a long period of marriage or after a number of female births in the family.

Men of the African Chaga tribe were reputed to block their anuses during the ceremony of attaining of manhood, to pretend that they did not defecate at all. This was also thought to be one way of establishing superiority over women.

Paris was once famous for its *pissoirs*, in which users were entirely visible to passers-by, except for a narrow screen at waist height. There used to be a British ferry poster with the slogan

'HARWICH FOR THE CONTINENT'

under which graffiti-writers would often scrawl

'PARIS FOR THE INCONTINENT'.

About a third of Americans flush
while they are still sitting on the toilet.

Seven billion gallons of water
are flushed down toilets in the U.S.
every day.

40,000 Americans are injured by
toilets every year.

Toilets in Australia flush counter clockwise.

◆

Alaska has the most outhouses of any US state.

Though the challenge to provide toilet facilities has been totally overcome in rich countries, it has still to be met in developing countries like India. The journey of the toilet has all but ended in Europe and North America, but it continues in the developing world.

During the late Middle Ages, the French invented the bidet for both sexes (obviously, the original models did not have modern plumbing). However, during WWI the main places British and American troops found them was in brothels, leading them to assume that they were only used by women. To this day, there are few men who use them.

MADE IN THE USA

Americans have had their own part to play in the development of the toilet. Thomas Jefferson, for example, devised an indoor privy at his Monticello home by rigging up a system of pulleys. Servants used the device to haul away chamber pots in his earth closet (a wooden box enclosing a pan of wood ashes below, and a seat with a hole cut out at the top). An architect and inventor, as well as a statesman, Jefferson also built two octagonal outhouses at his retreat at Poplar Forest in Virginia.

Conf-loo-sing!

When the colonists packed for the New World, they probably tucked a chamberpot in among other crockery items and tinware. But the use of the euphemistic term "chaise percee" or "commode" often confused the young immigrants. In the early 1800s, a settler's wife reportedly bought several from the new stock at the local store for kitchen and table use.

◆

The first American patent for a plunger closet is attributed to William Campbell and James T. Henry in 1857. It resembled the twin-basin water closets deplored by the great English engineer, S.S. Hellyer. The mechanism was unsanitary.

◆

◆

William Smith developed a jet
siphon closet in 1876. It was
carried still further by the famous
American sanitary engineer George
E. Waring, Jr, into larger and more
complicated pieces of sanitary
ware.

◆

Thomas Kennedy, another American, patented a siphonic closet which required only two delivery pipes, one to flush the rim, the other to start the siphon. William Howell improved it in 1890, when he eliminated the lower trap without detriment to the action.

Ten years later, Robert Frame and Charles Neff of Newport, R.I., produced the prototype of America's siphonic wash-down closet, although it sometimes failed to develop the necessary action and the contents overflowed. Another decade would pass before a redesigned bowl by Fred Adee would spur the production of the siphonic closet in America.

◆

In the early 1840s, the architect and designers of New York City's Central Park denounced the out-house as 'troublesome, unhealthy, indelicate, and ugly.' They tried to correct this by designing little Gothic structures combining a summer-house with a view of the garden on one side, and a two or four holer on the other.

◆

*O*ther than in a few private homes, hotels were the true bastions of luxury and comfort – and indoor plumbing. In 1829, a brilliant young architect, twenty-six year old Isaiah Rogers, inspired awe and envy throughout the country with his innovative Tremont Hotel in Boston. It was the first hotel to have indoor plumbing and became the prototype of a modern first-class American hotel.

However, in 1834 in New York City, Rogers surpassed his previous achievement in the Tremont House. He built the Astor House with six storeys, featuring seventeen rooms on the upper floors with water closets and bathrooms to serve 300 guest rooms. In the Tremont, water was drawn from a metal storage tank set on top of the roof, the recently invented steam pump raising the water on high. A simple water carriage system moved the excretal water to the sewerage system. As with other individual buildings of the time, each had its own source of water and removal.

◆

Nineteenth-century Americans were very fond of decorative toilets. Pedestal models proved most popular, highlighted with elaborate patterns and fanciful names. Popular examples were the English Lion and the Dolphin models. The Dolphin curled up into a letter S, the bowl in the shape of a fluted shell. (Carvings of dolphins had separated the seats used by the Roman soldiers in the privy at Timgad, an ancient Roman city in what is now Algeria).

A Dolphin water closet of Edward Johns & Co. won a Golden Award for design at the Great Philadelphia Exhibition in 1876. (The company today, Armitage Shanks, has reproduced the original 'Dolphin Suite' complete with mahogany toilet seat, vanity doors and polished brass taps and fittings.)

◆

Even as late as the end of the nineteenth century, it proved tough to convince Americans to buy American products. The pottery maker and decorator Thomas Maddock, an innovator in the American sanitary industry, came up with the idea of stamping each closet with a lion and a unicorn, and the following inscription: 'Best Stafford Earthenware made for the American market'.

ON THE THRONE

Visitors to the Palace of Versailles during the reign of Louis XIV would pay to be in the presence of the King, enabling them to witness his final royal movement of the day.

Queen Victoria was once being shown around Cambridge University where the town sewers discharged straight into the River Cam. She turned to her guide and questioned him about the pieces of paper floating in the river. As cool as a cucumber, he replied, 'Those, ma'am, are notices that bathing is forbidden.'

The Saxon king Edmund Ironside was murdered in 1016 while using the loo. An ancient chronicle records that he was 'struck with a spear in the fundament while at the withdraught to purge nature'.

*T*he French kings, Louis XIII and Louis XIV, used to give audience while using the toilet. Louis XIV had a commode under his throne, which prompted his court jester to remark that he found it a bit strange that, while the King preferred to eat in private, he chose to ease himself in public.

*T*he Great House of Easement was at King Henry VIII's palace at Hampton Court. It featured 28 seats on two different levels and was much appreciated by the King's courtiers. However, there was no flushing system and so a team of small boys had to crawl along the drains under the palace moat in order to perform the unenviable task of cleaning the royal loos.

King Henry VIII had his own portable loo known as a 'close stool'. His was a particularly fancy one – the box was upholstered in expensive black velvet, trimmed with silk ribbons and fringes and studded with 2,000 gold nails. His stool rooms were supervised by the 'Groom of the Stool', a much sought-after position given to a high-ranking courtier.

In 1844 no fewer than 53
overflowing cesspits were found
under Windsor Castle.

The late Diana,
Princess of Wales, decorated her
loo at Kensington Palace with
cartoons of her ex-husband.

During the Great Plague of 1666, King Charles II left London for Oxford to avoid infection. The Oxford diarist Anthony Wood described the King and his entourage thus: 'They were very nasty and beastly, leaving at their departure their excrements in every corner, in chimneys, studies, colehouses, cellars.'

TO WIPE OR NOT TO WIPE...

Instead of toilet paper, people in
ancient Rome used a piece of
sponge fixed to the end of a stick.
Wealthy ladies, however, preferred
to use an ostrich feather.

*T*he first paper specifically made for the toilet was manufactured in America in 1857 by the Joseph C. Gayetty Company of New Jersey. It was marketed as 'Gayetty's Medicated Paper – a perfectly pure article for the toilet and for the prevention of piles.'

Such was the prudery of the Victorians that selling toilet paper proved to be a difficult task. Chemists would stock it but only under the counter. To display it was considered very daring. Customers could not bring themselves to order it by name, preferring to use the euphemism 'curl papers' instead.

In nineteenth-century America, copies of the Sears catalogue would often be found in the toilet serving two purposes – as reading material and as wiping material (definitely in that order!).

In Romania the value of currency fell so low that toilet paper was made from five tons of shredded bank notes.

*T*oilet paper is used by a small minority of the world's population. Alternatives used are water, hands, newspapers or magazines, leaves, stones, feathers, corn cobs, rope, sticks, sand, old cloth and necks of geese (preferably dead ones).

Andrex, a very popular British brand of toilet paper, is named after St Andrew's Mill in Walthamstow, where it was invented in 1936. It was originally a hankie for gentlemen and was sold exclusively in Harrods.

A toilet-paper survey conducted in the USA by the Scott Paper Company revealed that ⅔ of people with a Master's or doctorate degree reported reading on the loo. 54% of those surveyed reported that they folded the tissue neatly before wiping; 35% just wad it into a ball to wipe.

The market for toilet paper in the UK is worth over £600 million annually. The average household uses 159 rolls, or about ¾ of a mile of paper per year. The average American uses more than twice as much as the average Briton.

Another word for
toilet paper is bumf, which is short
for bum fodder.

A company in North Carolina
produces a toilet-paper holder
that speaks. When the paper
is rolled, the holder says
'Yuk-yuk, stinky-stinky, nice one'.

The average tear of toilet paper is
5.90 sheets.

44% wipe from front to back from
behind their backs.

60% look at the paper after
they wipe.

42% fold, 33% crumple, 6% wrap it
around their hands.

50% say that they have wiped
with leaves.

8% say that they have wiped with
their hands.

2% have wiped
with money.

Some people believe that the tradition of shaking hands with the right hand has its origins in the Islamic tradition of wiping with their left hand. In Western cultures, it was thought that the left hand was therefore dirty!

In the days before toilet paper, where you lived helped to determine what you would use to wipe. Mussel shells were very popular in coastal regions before the twentieth century.

SPENDING A PENNY

'Plenty of Urine made in the Night, signifies but small Evacuations by Stool.'

Hippocrates: *Aphorisms*, Section 4, Aphorism LXXXIII

In medieval England some people used their own urine as an early-morning mouthwash.

In ancient Rome, the urine from public latrines was collected and used to help remove grease from clothes.

'We ought to inspect those things that proceed out of the Bladder, whether they are such as proceed from healthy Persons. For the more unlike they are to these, the more unhealthy are they; but the more they appear like the Urines of sound Bodies, the less diseased they argue the Party to be by whom they are made.'

Hippocrates: *Aphorisms*, Section 7, Aphorism LXVI

An Egyptian pharaoh with an eye infection is reported to have had it cured by the application of the urine of a woman, whom he later married.

◆

In certain circles there was a belief that the urine of a eunuch could help make women fertile.

It used to be thought that bathing your legs in warm urine was a cure for chilblains.

At St Paul's School in London in the seventeenth century, the boys' urine was collected and sold to tanners and dyers. The profits went to school funds.

VIEW FROM THE LOO

Judy Garland, Elvis Presley, Evelyn Waugh and King James I of Scotland all died sitting on the loo.

First published in 1929, Charles Sale's book about a carpenter who builds outdoor privies, *The Specialist*, is still in print and has sold over 1.5 million copies.

It may be called spending a penny but if you are caught short in Harrods, using the Knightsbridge store's facilities will cost you £1.00.

◆

There was a public notice in a field between Hove and Portslade which read, 'This place may not be used for that purpose.'

The public toilet in North Berwick in Scotland was declared the cleanest in Great Britain in 1994.

It has a guest book for visitors to sign and a Christmas tree in December.

*T*he town council of Cheltenham Spa once voted to replace the words 'Men' and 'Women' on some of the public lavatories with 'Gentlemen' and 'Ladies', in order to attract a better class of person.

There are several different theories as to the derivation of the word 'loo':

from the French word for water, *l'eau*

from the French word for place, *lieu*

from the word *ablution*

from the name *Luliana*

named after Lady *Louisa* Tennyson, daughter of the Earl of Lichfield

named after the French preacher, Louis *Bourdalou*.

On hearing that Elvis Presley had died while sitting on the loo, many of his loyal fans wanted to know, 'Was he reading the Bible?'

A team of American research psychologists have discovered that men's peeing habits in public toilets are affected by the proximity of their fellow peers (or pee-ers).

If someone is using the adjacent urinal, it delays the start of the average man's pee, and reduces his total peeing time by as much as 40%.

Kathleen Meyer, the American author of a useful outdoor handbook, is clearly a lady who believes in getting to the point quickly. The title of her book is *How to Shit in the Woods*.

For reasons of hygiene many women prefer to squat over toilet seats, rather than sit on them. A Californian company has invented La Funelle, a disposable coated paper funnel with a 12cm tube, which women can use to wee while standing up.

Several of London's Victorian public loos have now been converted for other purposes, ranging from a snooker hall to a children's nursery to a sandwich bar.

Anyone who worries about getting locked in a Superloo (more correctly called an Automatic Public Convenience) can be reassured. The door unlocks automatically at the beginning of the cleaning cycle or if a user has been in there for 17 minutes.

It has been recommended by dentists that a toothbrush be kept six feet away from a toilet to avoid airborne particles resulting from the flush.

Most toilets flush in E flat!

LOO-PHEMISMS

THE TOILET (n.)

Bog	Dyke
Boghouse	The Gents
Can	Holy of Holies
Cloakroom	Jakes
Closet	Jericho
Comfort room	John
Dunny	Khazi

The Ladies	Powder room
Lav	Privy
Little boys' room	Proverbial
Little girls' room	Rest room
Loo	Retiring place
Necessary house	Shady place
Netty	Shit-house
Place of easement	Smallest room
Place of repose	Thinking place
	Throne
	Thunderbox
	WC

GO TO THE TOILET (vb)

Answer the call
of nature
Be excused
Check on the
scones
Do the
necessary
Ease yourself
Explore the
geography of
the house

Find a haven of
refuge
Freshen up
Go into retreat
Go to Egypt
Go to the library
Go to your
private office
Lay some cable
Mail a letter

Pay a visit to
  your uncle
Pick a rose
Powder your
  nose
Relieve yourself
See a man about
  a horse
See your aunt
Shoot a dog
Shoot a lion

Use the
  cloakroom
Use the facilities
Visit Sir John
Visit the
  bathroom
Visit the old
  soldiers' home
Wash your
  hands

URINATE (vb)

Burn the grass
Do a number
  one
Drain the
  radiator
Drain the snake
Drain the spuds
Go and feed the
  goldfish
Go for a gypsy's
  kiss

Go for a tinkle
Go tap a kidney
Go to fix the
  plumbing
Go to plant a
  sweet pea
Have a slash
Kill a snake
Pass water
Pump ship
Relieve yourself

Shake the dew
    off the lily
Shake hands
    with an old
    friend
Shake hands
    with the vicar
Shed a tear
Spend a penny
Spring a leak
Squeeze the
    lemon

Take a leak
Tap a keg
Visit the green
    man
Water the crops
Water the
    dragon
Water the horses
Water the lawn
Worship at the
    altar

DEFECATE (vb)

Do ah-ahs
Do a George
Do a heap
Do a jobby
Do a job for
    yourself
Do a number
    two
Do a poo
Do ca-ca

Do your
    business
Have a shit
Lay a log
Make little
    soldiers
Move one's
    bowels
Take a crap
Take a dump

URINE (n.)

Jimmy Riddle	Piss
Number One	Wazz
Pee	Wee
Piddle	Widdle

EXCREMENT (n.)

Crap	Number Two
Dump	Poo
Jobby	Shit

FLUSHED WITH EXCITEMENT

THE LATEST TOILET INNOVATIONS

Thanks to a South African innovation in 2001, one of the few remaining differences between the sexes could now be eradicated. The 'Eezeewee', which has a reusable cup and length of pipe is designed to enable women to use urinals, looks set to finally cut those long queues for the ladies'.

In their bid to do their bit for the environment, in 2001 Los Angeles water chiefs came up with a 'toilet to tap' scheme. They planned to recycle billions of gallons of sewage waste into tap water.

Good news for all cat lovers. An American company have developed a self-cleaning litter box, which attaches to your home's drainage, dispensing with the need to clear up after your kitty.

*T*ourist officials in Rio de Janeiro have come up with a novel idea to deal with the stream of visitors who have been using the city as a giant open urinal. They have decided to spray Rio's 850 squares with strawberry perfumed water to combat the smell of urine.

PRIVY HUMOUR

Jokes from the John

What is the difference between a
toilet and a barman?

*A toilet only has to deal with one
arsehole at a time!*

How can you spot an
Irish aeroplane?

It's got an outside loo.

How many men does it take to
change a roll of toilet paper?

When it happens, we'll let you know.

Why don't men have to
use toilet paper?

*Because God made them
perfect arseholes.*

◆

Why is that boy hiding under
the bed?

*Because he thinks he's
a little potty.*

Gentlemen's Graffiti

Here I lie in stinky vapour
because some bastard stole the
toilet paper. Shall I lie or shall
I linger or shall I be forced
to use my finger…?

Everyone pisses on the floor.
Be a hero: shit on the ceiling.

(Written high on the loo wall)
*'If you can pee above this line, the fire
department wants you.'*

(Written over a urinal)
'Look up. Look up.'

(Written even higher on the wall)
'Keep looking up. Keep looking up.'

(Written on the ceiling)
*'Quick, look down!
You're peeing on your shoes!'*

Written above a men's urinal:

'Why are you looking up here?
Are you ashamed of it?'

Along the bottom of the partition
between cubicles in a public loo:

'Beware limbo dancers!'

Underneath a notice in a men's
public loo saying

'Please adjust your dress before leaving,'

someone had scrawled,

'If I could do that, I'd be in the ladies'.

◆

In this land of sun and sea,
Please don't flush for just one pee.

Signs in the smallest room

Sign above a loo:

'If you want a wet surprise
pull the chain before you rise!'

A sign in the London
Underground:

'Gents and Lift out of order:
Please use stairs.'

Sign in a public loo:

'We aim to please. You aim too. Please!'

Sign in a loo in a pub:

*'Please don't throw cigarette
butts in our urinal.
We don't piss in your ashtrays.'*

Sign on a loo door

*'Patrons are requested to remain seated
throughout the performance.'*

10 *Things to do in a public toilet*

1 Compliment people on their shoes.

2 Introduce yourself to the person in the next stall.

3 Scream, 'Oh my GOD! What the hell is THAT?'

4 Roll Easter eggs under the doors.

5 Ask whether anyone can see your pet river python.

6 Put clingfilm over the toilet bowl.

7 Write essay questions on the toilet paper.

8 Fake an orgasm.

9 Replace the roll of toilet paper with a roll of sandpaper.

10 Leave a fried egg floating in the bowl.

The good old days

In the days of old
When knights were bold
And toilets weren't invented,
They left their load
On the side of the road
And walked off so contented.

Other Little Books published by
Michael O'Mara Books Limited:

The Little Book of Gay Gags – ISBN 1-85479-590-2

The Little Book of Irish Grannies' Remedies –
ISBN 1-85479-828-6

The Little Book of Scottish Grannies' Remedies –
ISBN 1-85479-829-4

The Little Book of Irish Wit and Wisdom –
ISBN 1-85479-827-8

The Little Book of Scottish Wit and Wisdom –
ISBN 1-85479-826-X

The Little Book of the SAS – ISBN 1-85479-807-1

101 Really Unpleasant Things About Men –
ISBN 1-85479-881-2

Get Your Coat – You've Pulled – ISBN 1-85479-891-X

The Little Book of Crap Advice- ISBN 1-85479-883-9

The Little Book of Crap Excuses – ISBN 1-85479-882-0

The Little Book of Totally Stupid Men – ISBN 1-85479-833-2

The Little Couch Potato Book – ISBN 1-85479-834-0

Welcome to Dumpsville! – ISBN-1-85479-880-4

The Little Book of Despair – ISBN 1-85479-818-9

The Little Book of Tantric Sex For Busy People –
ISBN 1-85479-685-2

The Little Book of Sex Fantasies – ISBN 1-85479-725-5

All Michael O'Mara titles are available by post from:

Bookpost, PO Box 29, Douglas, Isle of Man IM99 1BQ

Credit cards accepted. Please telephone 01624-836000
fax: 01624-837033
Internet http://www.bookpost.co.uk
e-mail: bookshop@enterprise.net

Free postage and packing in the UK. Overseas
customers allow £1 per book (paperbacks) and
£3 per book (hardbacks).